Fafa

Fafa's Swimming Pool

Published by
Hughton Books and Publishers. Brampton Ontario, Canada
www.hughtonbooks.com

Printed in the U.S.A.

Summary: A young girl in Denu describes her town's relationship with the ocean and daily life by the coast of the Atlantic.

ISBN: 978-1-0689376-1-3

This book is dedicated to the men and women who labour along the coastlines. Our fishing families work tirelessly to safeguard and preserve the ocean.

__Ablavi De Souza

This book is dedicated to all the children who help their parents with chores, and still enjoy their childhood

__King David Hughton

HUGHTON
Books and Publishing
www.hughtonbooks.com

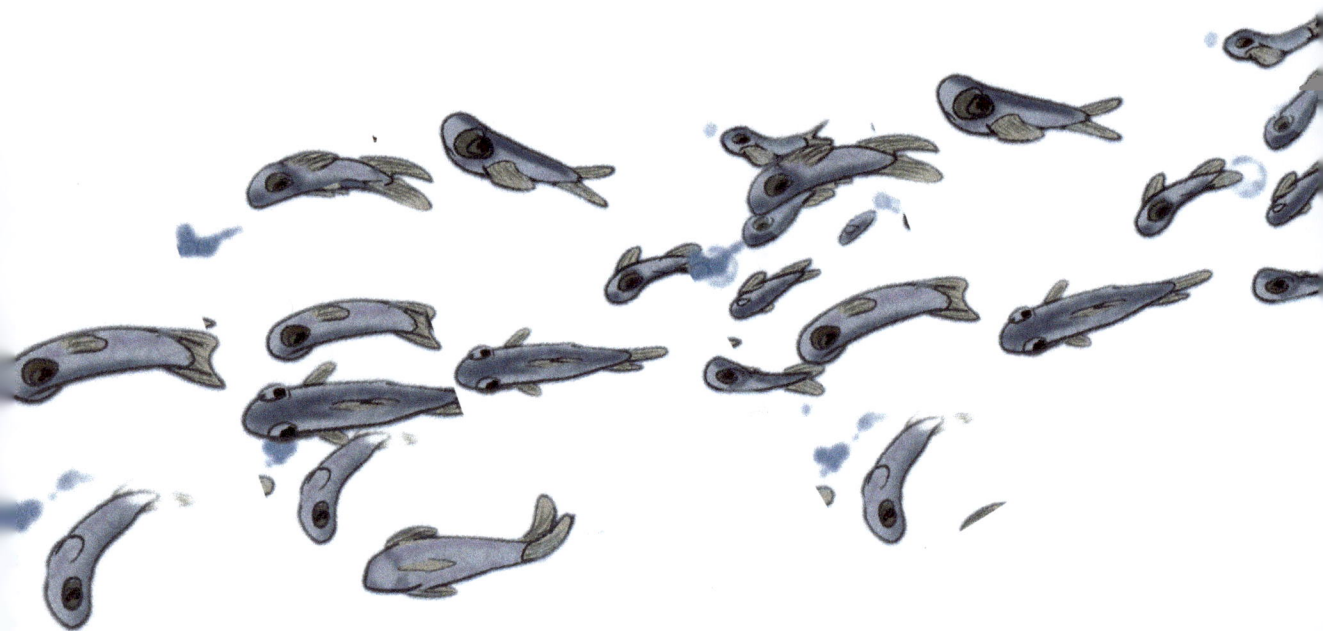

Fafa's Swimming Pool

Written by
Ablavi De Souza

Illustrated by
Kingdavid Hughton

This book belongs to:

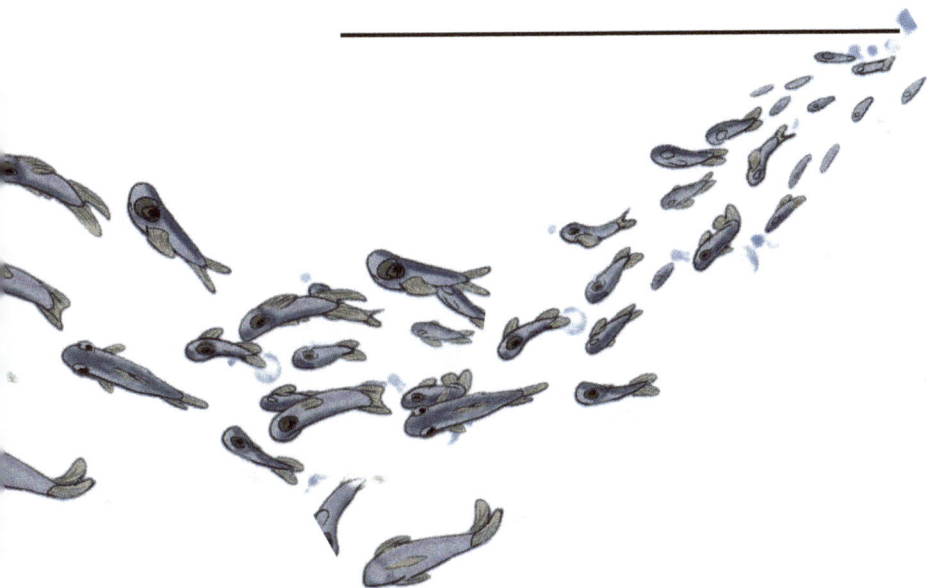

_____

Hi friends. My name is Fafa. I live in a town in Ghana called Denu, which has the most gigantic swimming pool in the whole wide world.

You see, our swimming pool is not inside a building but outside our house. Papa tells me that this big swimming pool is called the Atlantic Ocean, and our house is on the ocean's shore.

I love swimming in our gigantic pool. Most days after school, my brother, Nunya, and I grab some snacks, help Mama prepare dinner, and dive into the big waters. The ocean welcomes us with wide, open arms.

On days that the ocean is upset, Papa warns us to stay away. He says not to enter the sea when the strong wind and the waves are big because the waters could be fighting an angry storm.

Papa likes to swim with us. Sometimes, he watches us swim. He calls himself
'*The Lifeguard* and
The Caretaker
of the Giant Waters.'

We swim until we are tired or need to use the bathroom. Then Papa reminds us to take care of the ocean so the ocean will take care of us.

On weekends, our neighbours Ami, Elorm, and Yayra come to swim with us. At other times, when there is a picnic, others from the community also come to swim with us.

After all the fun games, Papa tells us to pick up all the rubbish we made before leaving the shores of our gigantic swimming pool.

Papa has taught us how to swim like the biggest fish in the waters—the whale. Papa loves telling stories about whales. This makes my brother want to swim like a giant whale.

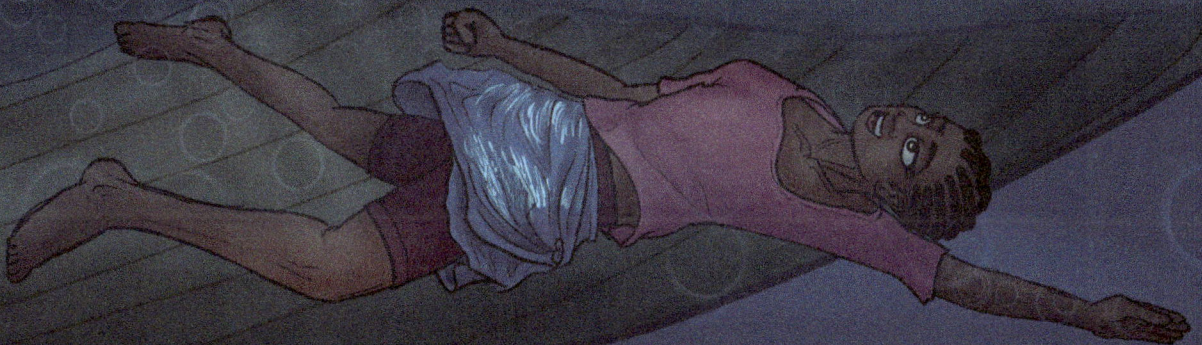

12

HeeeHo

ChoooBoyi

Papa once said he
and his friends
trapped a whale in
their fishing net
before our house.

The entire community
came to help free the
whale from the fishing
net.

13

The whale happily waved them goodbye as it returned home to the ocean. Today, Papa and his fishing friends use special nets that catch small fish, not whales.

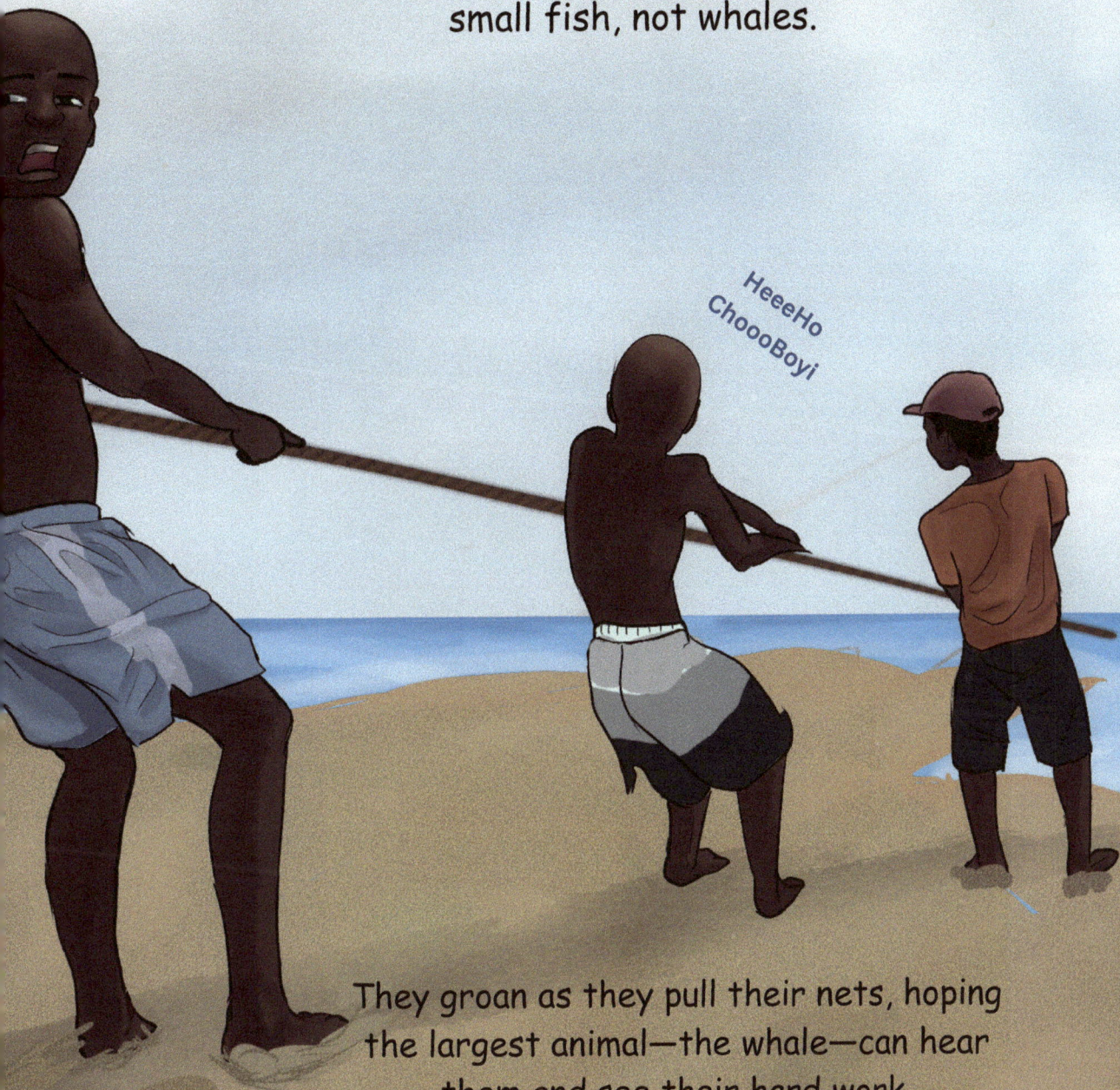

HeeeHo
ChoooBoyi

They groan as they pull their nets, hoping the largest animal—the whale—can hear them and see their hard work.

Some fish they catch now are Aborbi, herring, and sardines. Sometimes, their nets trap mackerels. A few days ago, Papa's net caught shrimps and a giant octopus! The octopus was not happy to be caught in the net.

Mama is happy when Papa's net catches shrimp because she says the ocean loses most of its fish.

When we bring our fish home, my brother and I help wash the sand and dirt off them. Then, we lay them out on different baskets under the sun to dry a little before Mama cooks them.

18

Mama is super good at making smoky fish. After the oven heats up, she places the fish in the clay oven. We all help out. Papa carries the remaining fish basket to the clay oven. My brother and I love fetching firewood for Mama to use.

Mama checks the fish every few minutes to ensure they cook well. She turns them over and over until they look nice and brown. We all watch the fish for Mama.

When the fish are well cooked, Mama removes them from the oven to cool down. Then, she puts them in bags and baskets for the market.

Market days are very busy in
Denu. People from different places
come to buy and sell.

Mama carries her fish to trade in the market, too. Her stall is located alongside other fish sellers from the community, as well as those from around the country and across the border from Togo, Benin, and Nigeria.

My brother, Nunya, and I go to Mama's stall after school on market days. Mama buys us snacks to eat. We love the sweet waters from fofonu - sugarcane. After eating and doing our homework in the market, we help Mama count the money she makes from selling the fish.

We are all happy when Mama sells all the fish she takes to the market. Papa always says that selling every fish basket means the world has food, which is something to celebrate.

The Ocean has been good to us. So, before bed every night, I look out my window at our big swimming pool and say, "Thank you, ocean, for giving us fish. Good night, big waters."

As usual, it responds in waves and whispers,
saying, "Good night, Fafa."

The End

Ablavi L. de Souza is an author of children's books. In addition to her authorship work, Ms. De Souza is an educator and the founder of the non-profit organization AfriCanada Hub. She seeks creative ways to bridge educational gaps between children from marginalized communities and their counterparts. Her work in the community has been characterized by an adept love of reading children's books with and to children. Outside her professional life, Ms. de Souza loves to pray, watch movies, drink tea, and try out new recipes.

Author

Kingdavid Hughton is a true artist, excelling not only as a concept artist and illustrator but also as a dedicated student. Drawing, writing and doing artistic work are integral to his identity—a passionate calling that flows through his very being.
Aside from school or his artwork, you'll find him writing stories, sharing vibrant moments, playing video games with friends, going for walks, or enjoying his other passion—cooking in the kitchen.

Illustrator

www.ingramcontent.com/pod-product-compliance
Lightning Source LLC
Chambersburg PA
CBHW040253100426
42811CB00011B/1252